THE CLEVELAND BROWNS

BY THOMAS K. ADAMSON

EPIC

BELLWETHER MEDIA ★ MINNEAPOLIS, MN

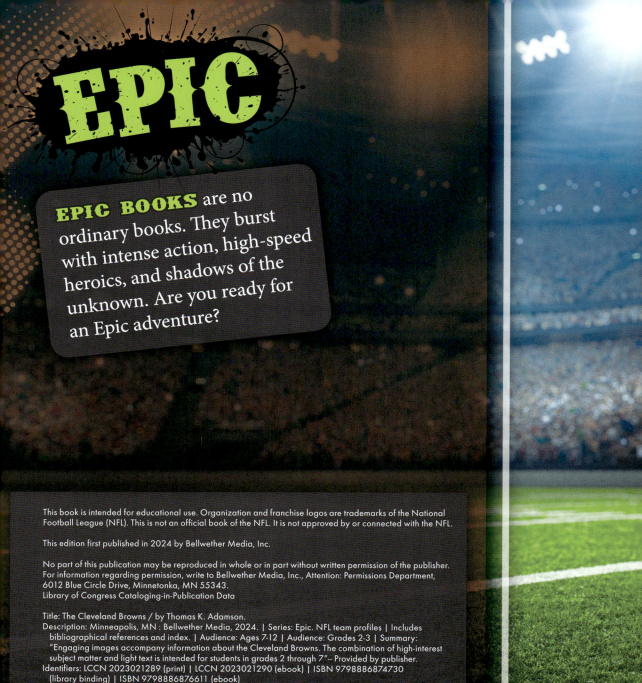

EPIC

EPIC BOOKS are no ordinary books. They burst with intense action, high-speed heroics, and shadows of the unknown. Are you ready for an Epic adventure?

This edition first published in 2024 by Bellwether Media, Inc.

Library of Congress Cataloging-in-Publication Data

Title: The Cleveland Browns / by Thomas K. Adamson.
Description: Minneapolis, MN : Bellwether Media, 2024. | Series: Epic. NFL team profiles | Includes bibliographical references and index. | Audience: Ages 7-12 | Audience: Grades 2-3 | Summary: "Engaging images accompany information about the Cleveland Browns. The combination of high-interest subject matter and light text is intended for students in grades 2 through 7"-- Provided by publisher.
Identifiers: LCCN 2023021289 (print) | LCCN 2023021290 (ebook) | ISBN 9798886874730 (library binding) | ISBN 9798886876611 (ebook)
Subjects: LCSH: Cleveland Browns (Football team : 1999-)--History--Juvenile literature. | Cleveland Browns (Football team : 1946-1995)--History--Juvenile literature.
Classification: LCC GV956.C6 A33 2024 (print) | LCC GV956.C6 (ebook) | DDC 796.332/640977132--dc23/eng/20230508
LC record available at https://lccn.loc.gov/2023021289
LC ebook record available at https://lccn.loc.gov/2023021290

Editor: Elizabeth Neuenfeldt   Designer: Gabriel Hilger

Printed in the United States of America, North Mankato, MN.

TABLE OF CONTENTS

FUMBLE RECOVERY!

The Browns face the Steelers in the 2021 **playoffs**. The ball flies past the Steelers' **quarterback**. It rolls into the **end zone**.

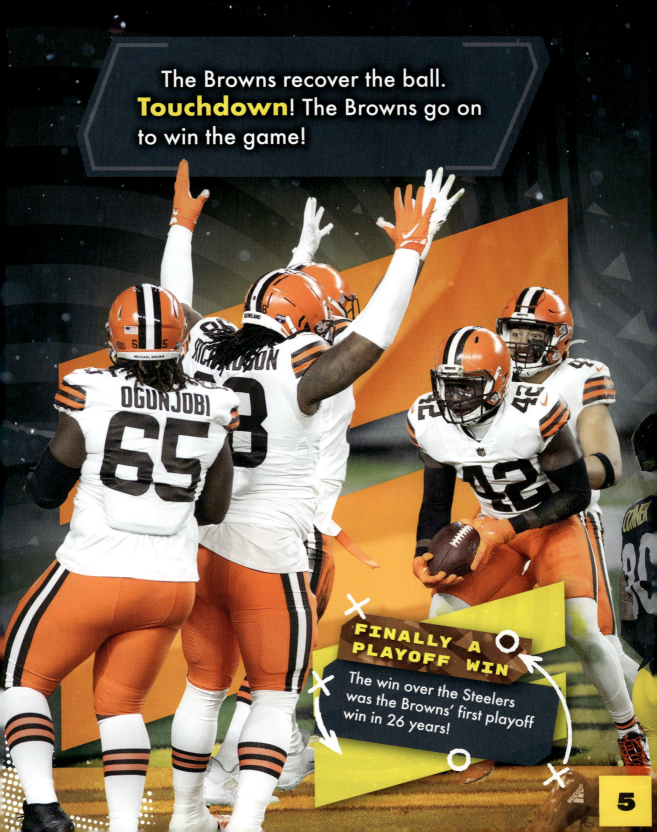

The Browns recover the ball. **Touchdown**! The Browns go on to win the game!

FINALLY A PLAYOFF WIN

The win over the Steelers was the Browns' first playoff win in 26 years!

THE HISTORY OF THE BROWNS

The Cleveland Browns started in the All-America Football Conference (AAFC) in 1946. They won the **championship** in each of this league's four seasons.
In 1950, the Browns joined the National Football League (NFL). They won the championship in their first season!

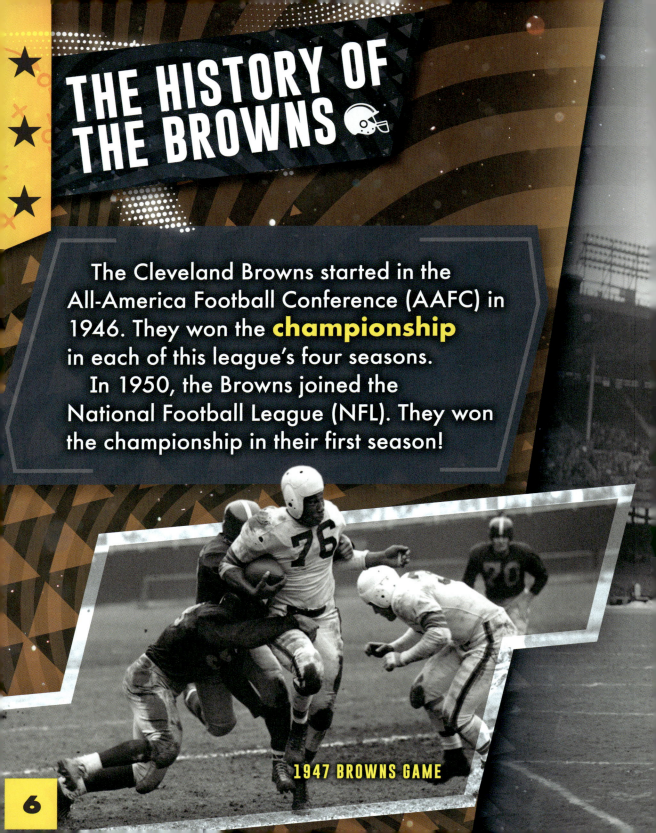

1947 BROWNS GAME

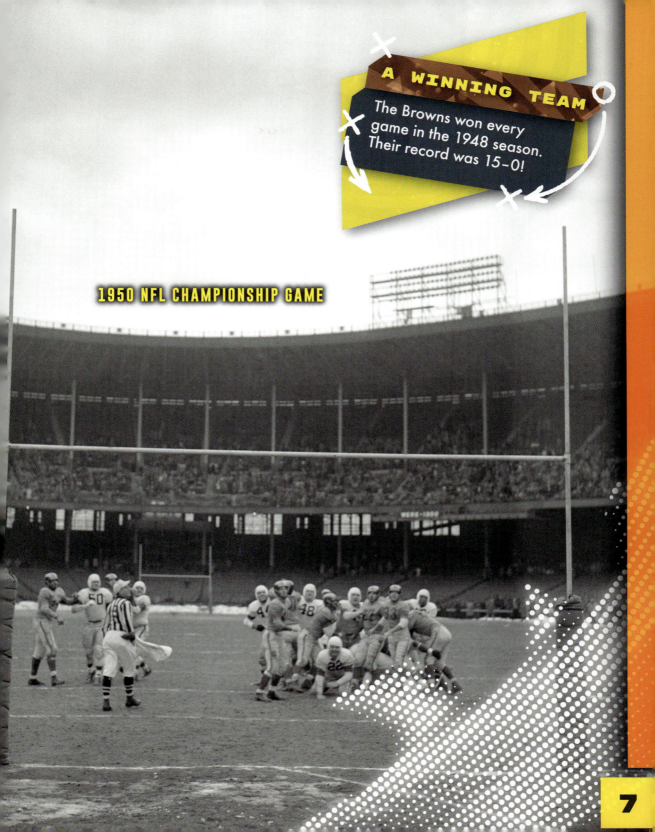

The Browns won every game in the 1948 season. Their record was 15–0!

1950 NFL CHAMPIONSHIP GAME

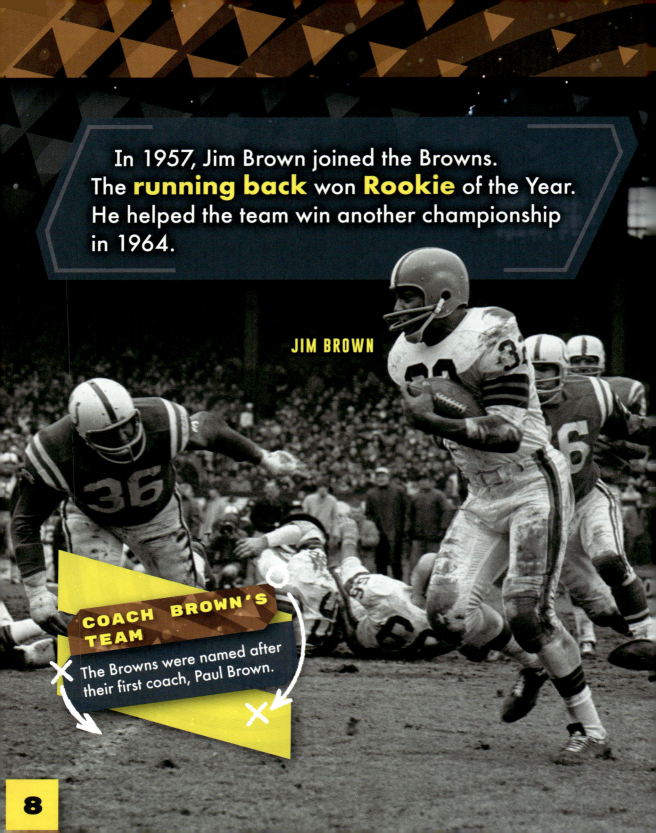

In 1957, Jim Brown joined the Browns. The **running back** won **Rookie** of the Year. He helped the team win another championship in 1964.

JIM BROWN

COACH BROWN'S TEAM

The Browns were named after their first coach, Paul Brown.

Brown helped the team reach the playoffs in 1965. But they lost.

The Browns missed the playoffs for most of the 1970s.

1978 BROWNS GAME

But they were one of the best teams of the 1980s. They went to the AFC Championship Game three times! But they lost all three games.

1987 AFC CHAMPIONSHIP GAME

11

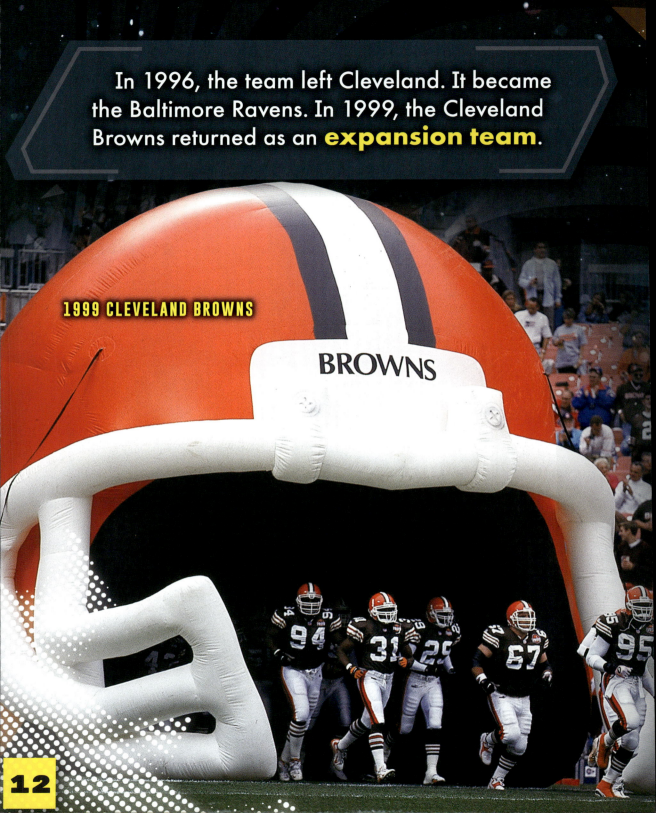

In 1996, the team left Cleveland. It became the Baltimore Ravens. In 1999, the Cleveland Browns returned as an **expansion team**.

1999 CLEVELAND BROWNS

BROWNS

They had many losing seasons. In 2020, Kevin Stefanski became head coach. He led the Browns to the playoffs!

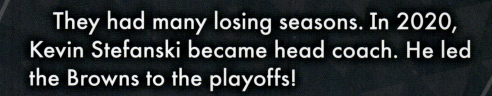

🏆 TROPHY CASE 🏆

NFL championships

4

AFC CENTRAL championships

6

NFL CENTURY championships

3

AAFC championships

4

THE BROWNS TODAY

BROWNS VS. STEELERS

The Browns play their home games at Cleveland Browns **Stadium**. It is in Cleveland, Ohio.

The team is part of the AFC North **division**. Their biggest **rival** is the Pittsburgh Steelers. This rivalry started in 1950.

📍 LOCATION 📍

CLEVELAND BROWNS STADIUM
Cleveland, Ohio

OHIO

GAME DAY!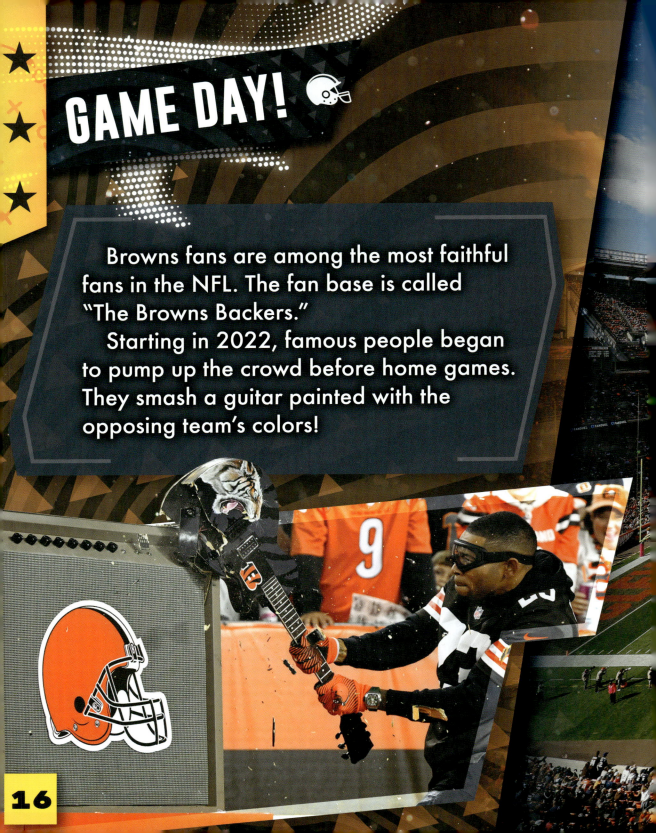

Browns fans are among the most faithful fans in the NFL. The fan base is called "The Browns Backers."

Starting in 2022, famous people began to pump up the crowd before home games. They smash a guitar painted with the opposing team's colors!

CLEVELAND BROWNS STADIUM

A section of seats near the end zone is called the Dawg Pound. The loudest fans fill this section.

Some fans wear dog masks. They bark and cheer for their team!

DAWG POUND

DAWG POUND

In 1985, players helped start the Dawg Pound. They barked when someone made a good play in practice. Fans took the "dawg" theme to games.

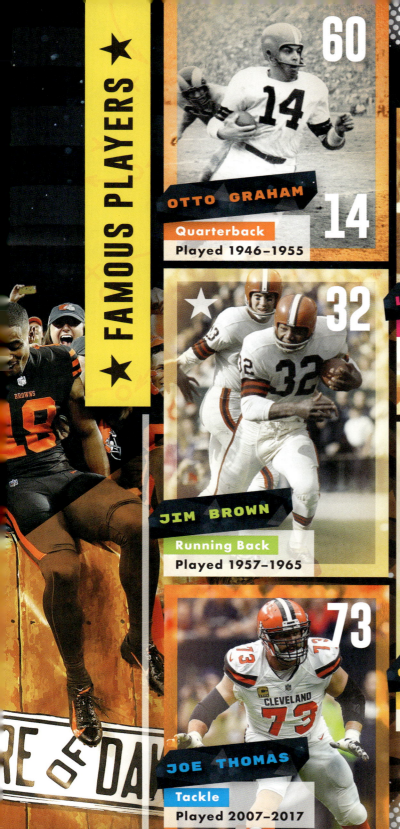

★ FAMOUS PLAYERS ★

60

14

OTTO GRAHAM
Quarterback
Played 1946–1955

32

JIM BROWN
Running Back
Played 1957–1965

73

JOE THOMAS
Tackle
Played 2007–2017

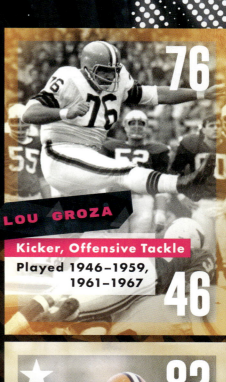

76

LOU GROZA
Kicker, Offensive Tackle
Played 1946–1959, 1961–1967

46

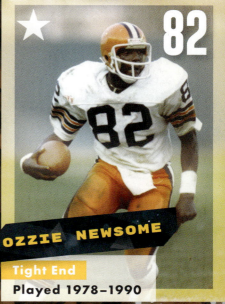

82

OZZIE NEWSOME
Tight End
Played 1978–1990

CLEVELAND BROWNS FACTS

LOGO

JOINED THE NFL | **1950**
(AAFC 1946–1949)

MASCOT

CHOMPS

NICKNAME | Dawgs

CONFERENCE
American Football
Conference (AFC)

COLORS

DIVISION | AFC North

Baltimore Ravens

Cincinnati Bengals

Pittsburgh Steelers

STADIUM

★ **CLEVELAND BROWNS STADIUM** ★
opened September 12, 1999

holds **67,895** people

⏰ TIMELINE

1950
The Browns join the NFL

1964
The Browns win their fourth NFL championship

1987
The Browns play in the AFC Championship Game

1996
The Browns move to Baltimore and become the Ravens

1999
Cleveland gets the Browns back as an expansion team

★ RECORDS ★

All-Time Scoring Leader	All-Time Rushing Leader	All-Time Receiving Leader	All-Time Passing Leader

 Lou Groza
1,608 points

Jim Brown
12,312 yards

 Ozzie Newsome
7,980 yards

Brian Sipe
23,713 yards

21

GLOSSARY

championship—a contest to decide the best team or person

division—a group of NFL teams from the same area that often play against each other; there are eight divisions in the NFL.

end zone—an area at either end of a football field; teams score points when they go into the end zone.

expansion team—a new team added to a sports league

playoffs—games played after the regular NFL season is over; playoff games determine which teams play in the championship game.

quarterback—a player whose main job is to throw and hand off the ball

rival—a long-standing opponent

rookie—a first-year player in a sports league

running back—a player whose main job is to run with the ball

stadium—an arena where sports are played

touchdown—a score that occurs when a team crosses into their opponent's end zone with the football; a touchdown is worth six points.

TO LEARN MORE

AT THE LIBRARY

Abdo, Kenny. *Cleveland Browns*. Minneapolis, Minn.: Abdo Zoom, 2022.

Fishman, Jon M. *Baker Mayfield*. Minneapolis, Minn.: Lerner Publications, 2021.

Whiting, Jim. *Cleveland Browns*. Mankato, Minn.: Creative Education, 2020.

ON THE WEB

FACTSURFER

Factsurfer.com gives you a safe, fun way to find more information.

1. Go to www.factsurfer.com.

2. Enter "Cleveland Browns" into the search box and click 🔍.

3. Select your book cover to see a list of related content.

INDEX